Michelangelo

Detail from Plate V-VI.

Funk & Wagnalls, Inc., New York

E. H. RAMSDEN

TRANSLATOR AND EDITOR OF
'THE LETTERS OF MICHELANGELO'

Michelangelo
1475-1564

1. THE DONI TONDO UFFIZI, FLORENCE

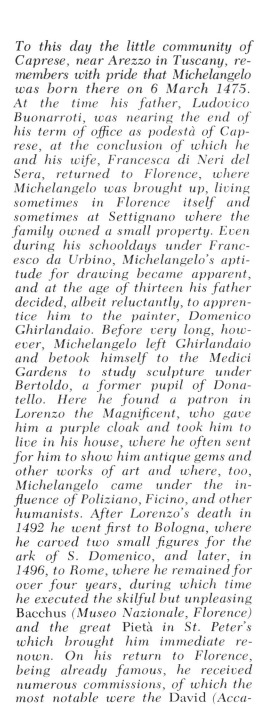

To this day the little community of Caprese, near Arezzo in Tuscany, remembers with pride that Michelangelo was born there on 6 March 1475. At the time his father, Ludovico Buonarroti, was nearing the end of his term of office as podestà of Caprese, at the conclusion of which he and his wife, Francesca di Neri del Sera, returned to Florence, where Michelangelo was brought up, living sometimes in Florence itself and sometimes at Settignano where the family owned a small property. Even during his schooldays under Francesco da Urbino, Michelangelo's aptitude for drawing became apparent, and at the age of thirteen his father decided, albeit reluctantly, to apprentice him to the painter, Domenico Ghirlandaio. Before very long, however, Michelangelo left Ghirlandaio and betook himself to the Medici Gardens to study sculpture under Bertoldo, a former pupil of Donatello. Here he found a patron in Lorenzo the Magnificent, who gave him a purple cloak and took him to live in his house, where he often sent for him to show him antique gems and other works of art and where, too, Michelangelo came under the influence of Poliziano, Ficino, and other humanists. After Lorenzo's death in 1492 he went first to Bologna, where he carved two small figures for the ark of S. Domenico, and later, in 1496, to Rome, where he remained for over four years, during which time he executed the skilful but unpleasing Bacchus *(Museo Nazionale, Florence) and the great* Pietà *in St. Peter's which brought him immediate renown. On his return to Florence, being already famous, he received numerous commissions, of which the most notable were the* David *(Acca-*

demia di Belle Arti, Florence), the Bruges Madonna *(Church of Notre-Dame, Bruges), the* Doni Tondo *(Uffizi, Florence) and the* Cascina Cartoon *(destroyed in 1512).*

In 1505, when much of what he had undertaken had scarcely been begun, he was summoned to Rome by Pope Julius II (1503-1513) and ordered to execute his tomb, which was conceived on so stupendous a scale that nothing less would suffice than the rebuilding of St. Peter's to accommodate it. This commission proved to be the great tragedy of Michelangelo's life. 'It is borne in upon me', he wrote, 'that I lost the whole of my youth chained to this tomb'. For forty years the work was constantly interrupted by other papal commissions until at last, when it was eventually erected in S. Pietro in Vincoli in 1545, it emerged as little more than a travesty of the original design, the Moses, *which had been all but completed thirty years before, being the only figure worthy of Michelangelo's genius. Ironically, also, it* never contained the Pope's remains. Between 1506 and 1508 he worked in Bologna *on the over life-size bronze of Julius II, which was set up on the façade of S. Petronio, but was thrown down by the Pope's enemies four years later; and between 1508 and 1512 he was engaged on the vault of the Sistine Chapel in Rome. Then in 1513 Julius died and Michelangelo's fortunes changed. During the pontificate of Leo X (1513-1521) he was commissioned to erect the façade of S. Lorenzo in Florence, which in turn involved opening up the marble quarries at Pietrasanta, but after four years intensive labour the contract was unexpectedly cancelled.*

Under Clement VII (1523-1534) who succeeded the Dutch Pope Adrian VI (1521-1523), Michelangelo was employed on the New Sacristy and the Medici tombs at S. Lorenzo. But the work was interrupted by political disasters, the sack of Rome in 1527 and the siege of Florence in 1529/1530, so that when he left Florence for good in 1534, following the fall of the Republic, the project was little more than half realized. For the new Pope, Paul III (1534-1549), who appointed him chief architect, sculptor and painter to the Vatican at a salary of 1,200 scudi a year, he painted The Last Judgment (Plate XI-XII) on the altar wall of the Sistine and the two frescoes in the Pauline Chapel, *The Conversion of St. Paul (Fig. 5) and The Crucifixion of St. Peter (Fig. 6), assignments which he accepted very unwillingly, because, as he said to Vasari, 'fresco is not work for old men'. In addition to these undertakings, which occupied him from 1536 to 1549, Michelangelo was also concerned with architectural schemes for the defence and embellishment of the city, while in 1547 the Pope prevailed upon him to accept the appointment of architect of St. Peter's. To this task, which he did not wish to undertake and which he knew he could not live to complete, he devoted the remaining seventeen years of his life, during the successive pontificates of Julius III (1550-1555), Marcellus II (1555), Paul IV (1555-1559), and Pius IV (1559-1565).* Architect, sculptor, painter and poet, he died in his house in Rome on 18 February 1564, honoured by his distinguished patrons, beloved by his friends and universally recognized as the greatest artist in the world.

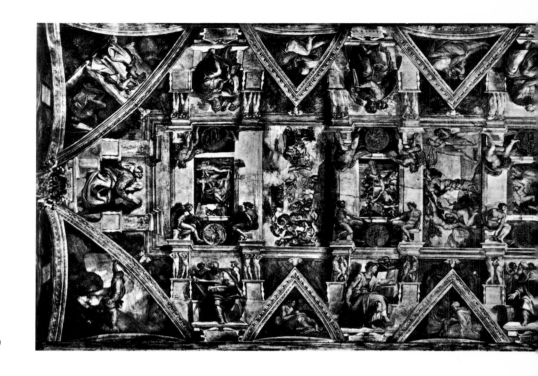

'Painting is a music and a melody.' MICHELANGELO

'Unique as a painter, superlative as an architect, Michelangelo always remained a sculptor at heart. 'Painting is not my profession', he used to say, and this his rivals, notably Bramante and Raphael, well believed. Thinking, therefore, on his return to Rome in 1508, to bring him into disrepute with Julius II, whose known regard for him was the occasion of much jealousy, they prevailed upon the Pope to set him to paint the vault of the Sistine Chapel, instead of permitting him to continue his work on the Julius Tomb, an enterprise in which he was bound to excel. Feeling himself unequal to the task, and pleading his ignorance of fresco, Michelangelo did everything in his power to reject the commission in favour of Raphael, but without avail. Julius remained obdurate and Michelangelo was left with no option but to obey.

HE WAS NOW thirty-three years of age. But while as a sculptor he already had four major works to his credit, as a painter he had had no comparable experience and knew little of fresco beyond what he may have learnt as an apprentice in Ghirlandaio's workshop. The only three easel pictures by his hand that have survived were, however, early works. Of these—the *Doni Tondo* (Fig. 1), *The Entombment* (Fig. 4) and the *Manchester Madonna* (Plate I)—only the first is documented as being by Michelangelo, although the second and the third, both unfinished, were attributed to him in the collections in which they were first recorded at the end of the seventeenth century. But while their authenticity was afterwards disputed, no convincing alternative hand has yet been proposed, each suggestion put forward having been, if that were possible, more banal than the last. And, indeed, how should it be otherwise? Technically, the two panels are interrelated; stylistically, *The Entombment* is allied to the *Doni Tondo*, in the frontal arrangement of the figures, in the type of the bearded head behind the Christ Child in the one and the dead Christ in the other, and also in the astringency of the colour harmonies; compositionally, the *Manchester Madonna* is akin to the carving of the *Bruges Madonna* (Church of Notre-Dame, Bruges), which belongs to the same period, in the compactness of its form, in the noble detachment of the Virgin, and in its pre-eminently sculptural design. But over and above

this, both pictures are characterized by a profound conviction and by a sublime austerity which places them in a category of their own and their authenticity, therefore, beyond all reasonable doubt, as many authorities now recognize. Yet masterly as they are, these early paintings are neither frescoes, nor such as to warrant the acceptance of a contract on the scale of the Sistine vault. No wonder, therefore, that Michelangelo was daunted.

Some notion of his reaction towards the task with which he found himself confronted may perhaps be gauged from a letter to his father about a family matter, written a year

2. LONG VIEW OF THE SISTINE CHAPEL, ROME

later. 'Above all', he wrote, 'whatever you do, do it without dismay, for there is no undertaking, however great, which, if undertaken without dismay, does not appear small'. Not that he himself had felt any undue confidence. On the contrary, only a few months before, when complaining about his lack of payment, he had added, 'I do not ask for anything because my work does not seem to me to go ahead in a way that merits it. This is owing to the difficulty of the work and because it is not my profession.'

THE SISTINE CHAPEL, built by Sixtus IV (1471-1484), an earlier della Rovere Pope and uncle of Julius II, is rather more than 130 feet long and 43 feet wide with the altar at the west end. The ceiling, which at its highest point rises to fifty-nine feet, is 'in the form of a barrel vault resting on lunettes, six to the length and two to the width of the building'. But while by the beginning of the Cinquecento the walls had already been enriched with frescoes by the foremost painters of Italy, the vault had been left without any comparable decoration, having been finished with nothing more appropriate than a spangle of gold stars on a blue background. But what the Pope got when Michelangelo had finished with it was literally more than he had bargained for—not what he had commissioned, not what he had anticipated, and certainly not what he paid for—namely, three hundred and forty-six figures for the price of twelve.

In a letter to a friend of his written some years later, Michelangelo explained the matter of the contract in these words: 'When I had set up the figure [the bronze of Julius II in Bologna] on the façade and returned to Rome, Pope Julius . . . set me to paint the vault of Sixtus and we made a bargain for three thousand ducats. The first design . . . was for twelve apostles in the lunettes and the usual ornaments to fill the remaining area. After the work was begun . . . I told the Pope that if the Apostles alone were put there it seemed to me that it would turn out a poor affair. He asked me why. I said, "because they themselves were poor". Then he gave me a new commission to do what I liked and said that he would content me.'

'To paint what he liked'—the prospect was tremendous; but first of all he had to acquire the art of fresco. This

he endeavoured to do with the aid of Francesco Granacci, Jacopo l'Indaco and other painters whom he summoned from Florence to assist him. But to little purpose; none of them was capable of doing what he required and after a short time he decided to proceed alone, or only with such help as his apprentices could give him.

Despite much speculation as to the origin of the theme or 'programme' for the vault and the source from which Michelangelo drew his initial inspiration, the problem has never been resolved. Vasari, who knew him intimately, makes no mention of a programme based on erudite theological allusions such as some pundits claim to have discovered in it, but which others (in the manner of the Lord) 'cannot away with'. Instead, Vasari speaks only of the artistic merits of a work which 'contains every perfection that can be given' and leaves all men stupefied. If, however, a prototype were to be sought, it seems possible that one would need to look no further than those bronze doors of the Baptistry in Florence, which Michelangelo himself once described as beautiful enough to be the Doors of Paradise. In any case, it is at least certain that in his choice of programme Michelangelo was using the iconographic idiom current in his time, and that, in the clarity of its definition, the design for the ceiling is conceived essentially in terms of sculpture, to which the notion of the niched and socled figure in an architectural setting, both real and contrived, is fundamental. The analogy between the framed reliefs of the doors and the four large and five smaller compartments into which the highest section of the vault is divided, as also between the alternating male and female figures bordering the reliefs and the alternating Prophets and Sibyls flanking the compartments is significant, no matter to what extent Michelangelo may subsequently have enlarged and adapted the theme.

Like Ghiberti's reliefs, these nine compartments are all devoted to Old Testament subjects. Beginning above the altar, the scenes represented in succession are, *The Division of Light from Darkness, The Creation of the Sun and Moon, The Separation of the Waters, The Creation of Adam* (Plate XVI), *The Creation of Eve, The Temptation and Expulsion* (Plate VIII), *The Sacrifice of Noah, The Deluge* (Plate IX) and *The Drunkenness of Noah.* And of these nine 'histories', as they are called, five are clearly reminiscent in principle of Ghiberti's handling of the same events. And particularly is this so in the case of *The Drunkenness of Noah*, a fact which renders the argument still more pertinent when one remembers that it was not with the compartments above the altar, but with those at the entrance that Michelangelo began his mighty undertaking.

Proceeding thus episodically in an inverse direction and gradually freeing himself from all precursive influences, he rapidly advanced from the more familiar earthbound events of the Biblical narrative towards the more remote, cosmic and sublime, until at last, and, as it were, in a creative onrush, he arrived at an overall achievement of unsurpassed splendour, might, majesty, and power.

UNWILLING THOUGH he had been to begin, once he had done so, he spared himself nothing during the four years that he devoted to the enterprise, despite the fact that he endured the utmost discomfort throughout, 'having to stand with his head thrown back', as described by Vasari and as depicted by himself in the rough sketch which accompanies his own sardonic lines —

I' ho già fatto un gozzo in questo stento.
(With this exertion have I grown a goitre).

During this period he only left Rome three times; once on a brief visit to Florence, and twice to Bologna in pursuit of Julius and the necessary ducats to enable him to re-erect the scaffolding after the uncovering of the first half of the ceiling in 1510.

In the sixteenth century the marble screen which divides the chapel stood nearer to the altar than it does today, immediately below *The Creation of Eve*, at the logical point of division between the histories of the Creation and those of the Fall. It was at this point, with the transcendent *Creation of Adam*, the most famous fresco in the world, that Michelangelo began work on the second half. Owing partly to the experience he had gained, and partly to the opportunity he had had of viewing the work from the ground when the scaffolding had been removed, he now developed a style of greater freedom, breadth and nobility, consonant at once with a profounder understanding of the requirements of the art of fresco, and a more exalted vision of his subject. But while this is true as far as the treatment of the histories is concerned, it is not true of the flanking figures of the Prophets and Sibyls, nor yet of the *Ignudi* (Nudes), which from the outset were realized with a monumentality and a grace that seem little short of miraculous.

Apart from the stupendous organization of the design, perhaps the most astonishing feature of the entire work, if one excellence may be preferred among so many, is the way in which a perfect balance is maintained between the unity of the composition as a whole, notwithstanding its complexity, and the elaboration of the parts, notwithstanding their diversity. While no component is lacking in its proper exposition, none is obtrusive. Similarly, the wealth of invention displayed in every detail is equalled only by the depth of perception and the range of

4. *THE ENTOMBMENT* NATIONAL GALLERY, LONDON

feeling manifested in every phase of the work. Nothing, for instance, could better exemplify Michelangelo's immense powers of observation and his intuitive grasp of the innermost differences between the young, clear-sighted and active, and the old, purblind and infirm than the variety of age, attitude and expression exhibited by the magnificent figures of the seven Prophets and five Sibyls enthroned with their attendants between the spandrels and at each end. But differentiated though they are as individuals, as a group they are yet united by the intensity of concentration by which each in turn is wrapt away into his own inner world.

Again, it would be difficult to imagine a more arresting contrast than that between the glory of God, the Father, the Creator, portrayed in the vault above, and the homeliness of the Ancestors of Christ, depicted in the spandrels and lunettes below — scenes of everyday life sympathetically observed and simply transcribed with all the tenderness of which Michelangelo was capable.

But of the many elements of which this incomparable work is made up, undoubtedly the most daring, perhaps the most beautiful, certainly the most original and the most Michelangelesque, is the frieze (if it may be so called) of the *Ignudi*, who, seated on plinths ranged at intervals along the painted cornices above the thrones of the Prophets and Sibyls, hold suspended the bronze medallions which terminate the five smaller compartments of the histories. In every variety of pose, the embodiment of a strange diversity of mood from the meditative to the gay, from the yearning to the turbulent, these youthful figures, some of which bear the della Rovere device of oak leaves and acorns, all of whom live immemorially a peculiar inward life of their own, represent Michelangelo's supreme aesthetic ideal as exemplified in terms of the human body.

ALTERNATELY IMPORTUNED and harassed by the Pope in his impatience to see the vault completed, Michelangelo toiled on; his mind set on the work, his body exhausted by the effort. 'Pray God my thing may end well', he wrote in a letter to his father in the spring of 1512, and in another to his brother Buonarroto, some three months later, 'I work harder than any man who ever lived. I'm not well and worn out with this stupendous labour and yet I'm patient in order to achieve the end desired' — and still later, again to Buonarroto, 'The truth is, it's so great a labour that I cannot estimate the time within a fortnight. Let it suffice that I shall be home for All Saints . . . if I do not die in the meantime.' Michelangelo did not die, but neither did he return to Florence for the family festival. Instead, he wrote to his father saying, 'I have finished the chapel I have been painting; the Pope is very well satisfied. But other things have not turned out for me as I'd hoped . . .'

On the eve of All Saints, 1512, vespers were sung in the Sistine Chapel to mark the completion of the painting of the vault. In an entry to this effect made in the Diary of the Papal Master of Ceremonies, Michelangelo's name was not recorded.

EXCEPT FOR the only other known easel picture by his hand, the ill-fated *Leda*, which eventually passed into the French Royal Collection but subsequently disappeared, some twenty-two years were to elapse before Michelangelo again turned his attention to painting. This time it was at the behest of Clement VII who desired him to paint the altar wall of the Sistine, an assignment which he had no wish to accept and of which he hoped to be quit when Clement died shortly afterwards. But the new Pope, Paul III, had no intention of relinquishing his services now that he was at last in a position to command them; and thus it was that in April or May 1536 Michelangelo began the painting of *The Last Judgment* (Plate XI-XII). Though in no sense as formidable an undertaking as the vault, the new fresco occupied him for a year longer and was not uncovered until 31 October 1541. But whereas formerly he had been sustained by the élan and the vigour of youth, he was now, at least physically, past his prime. If therefore, despite the subtlety of its organization and the force of its impact, *The Last Judgment* lacks the inner compulsion and creative urgency of the ceiling, just as it lacks its freedom, its sweep and, above all, its inevitability, who can wonder? At the same time and in all fairness, it must not be forgotten that the work is much spoilt by the ravages of time, candle-smoke and restoration, to say nothing of the tinkerings in his own lifetime of those who, having the temerity, in response to the question 'With what bodies do they come?', to reply 'Draped', caused sundry loincloths to be added. This affront Michelangelo bore with equanimity, *Pazienza!*

In one of his letters Vasari, speaking of him with much affection as *il mio raro e divinissimo Vecchio*, quoted him as saying that 'those who become the asses of princes early in life lay up for themselves a burden even beyond the grave'. And truly in his own experience this was the case. For scarcely had he finished *The Last Judgment* before Paul III prevailed upon him to undertake two large frescoes in his newly-built Pauline Chapel. During the seven years he was engaged on these the work was twice interrupted when, to the consternation of the whole of Rome, he appeared to be at the point of death. Yet, visibly tired though he was, he continued to pursue 'the desired end'. But at last the work drew to a close and on

5. *THE CONVERSION OF ST. PAUL*
PAULINE CHAPEL, THE VATICAN, ROME

13 October 1549, less than a month before the old Pope's death, Paul III mounted a ladder to inspect the second fresco which was then nearing completion. This second fresco, *The Crucifixion of St. Peter*, had occupied Michelangelo for eight hundred and seven days, only two days longer than the first, *The Conversion of St. Paul*. These paintings were his last contribution to an art which he had come to regard as second only to sculpture—'Painting', he is reputed to have said, 'is a music and a melody to be understood only by the intellect, and that with difficulty'.

6. *THE CRUCIFIXION OF ST. PETER*
PAULINE CHAPEL, THE VATICAN, ROME

I. MADONNA AND CHILD WITH ST. JOHN AND THE ANGELS (c. 1500)

Tempera on panel. 41½ in. x 30¼ in.
National Gallery, London

This unfinished painting is believed to be an example of Michelangelo's early work. Though there are no surviving preparatory sketches for this panel, there are similarities between the face of the Madonna here, and that of the *Bruges Madonna* and the *Pietà*, early sculptures for which drawings do exist.

The composition shows the Madonna and Child and little St. John at the centre. Four angels, standing in pairs at either side, are studying a song. The two angels at left are drawn in, ready to be painted. Both the two completed angels at the right and the Madonna reveal the young Michelangelo's search for sculptural form in figure and drapery. The completed angel nearest the Virgin bears a striking resemblance to a sketch of the young Michelangelo when he was an apprentice in Ghirlandajo's studio.

The olive-green tones of the Madonna's cape contrast with the orange-pinks of Her dress and the angels' tunics. The grey-blue drapery suggests the rounded shape of the knee beneath. Michelangelo's planned disorder of the clothing adds to the movement in the panel, as do the lively gestures of the Child and St. John. The brooding, contemplative expressions in this work suggest the mood in the later Sistine frescoes.

II. THE PROPHET ZACHARIAH (1508-10)
Fresco.
Vault of the Sistine Chapel, Rome

Zachariah's placement above the entrance to the chapel has particular importance because he refers to the coming of Christ (Zachariah 9:9) and the events of Palm Sunday. The Pope enters through this doorway on Palm Sunday after distributing palms to the people.

Behind Zachariah, and standing near most of the Prophets and Sibyls, are two guardian spirits (genii or cherubs) who assist in their meditations or inspirations, forming a link between God's voice and the action of these major figures.

One of the first characters Michelangelo painted on the perpendicular of the chapel entrance, Zachariah is seated in sharp profile, looking for a particular passage in his book. His figure, draped in wide folds, is struck by slanting rays of light. Zachariah's flatter dimensions are typical of Michelangelo's handling in earlier sections of the fresco. The artist harmonizes the rich red of the prophet's mantle with the soft green of his robe and his gold sleeve. There is an interesting contrast between the somewhat static pose of his head and his rhythmic flowing garments, indicating Michelangelo's awareness of the ceiling's dramatic possibilities.

ZACHERIAS

III. THE CUMAEAN SIBYL (1508-10)
Fresco.
Vault of the Sistine Chapel.

Michelangelo portrays this seeress as an old woman of somewhat sinister appearance. She seems not to be reading her book of prophecy so much as brooding on its contents. Cumaea was the most famous of Apollo's votaries, having sold her three Sibylline books to Tarquin, the last king of early Rome. The descendant of a mythic race of giants, she supposedly foretold the virgin birth of the Redeemer in the fourth of Virgil's Eclogues.

Here she is exaggeratedly muscular. Her large terra cotta body is clad in a lilac pink gown and draped with a gold ochre shawl. The form is sculptural, massive and dramatic. One of the two embracing cherubs at the left brings another book to satisfy her thirst for knowledge. These figures look on, concerned and attentive.

There is a continuous movement in the composition from the entwined arms of the cherubs through the powerful angle of the Sibyl's left arm. The curving draperies over her legs continue this flowing rhythm, contributing to Michelangelo's effect of suggesting the restraint of strongly charged emotions.

CVMAEA

IV. THE LIBYAN SIBYL; THE ANCESTORS OF CHRIST (1510-12)
Fresco.
Vault of the Sistine Chapel

The Libyan Sibyl, in Michelangelo's plan, lies just below the Lord separating Light from Darkness. She comes by this placement naturally because, according to Pausanius, she is the daughter of Zeus. Her mother was a sorceress, and thus her powers to foretell the future are inherited.

The Libyan Sibyl is one of the artist's most fully realized figures, as she turns gracefully, lifting her heavy book. She is about to rise. Her shoulders and arms are beautifully modelled. The lavender and gold of her tunic and robe are repeated in her Oriental turban. One of the cherubs turns away, repeating the profile, and gestures towards the Sibyl.

In the adjoining spandrel, as in seven others, a female figure dominates the composition. These forms are not identified, other than as the Hebrew forebears of Christ. All their expressions convey an air of expectancy or dread. In each case, Michelangelo has used the architectural form to create a niche where these figures dwell, performing their humble duties or, as shown here, posing gracefully in an expectant attitude.

LIBICA

V-VI. THE CREATION (1510-12)
Fresco.
Vault of the Sistine Chapel

The creation of the sun and the moon (at bottom) was executed first in this group. At the right, the figure of the Lord surges upward and with His imperious right hand assigns the sun to its place, then with His left, the moon. Angels attend Him, and one of them shields His eyes from the sun's brilliance. God's figure hurries away at the left, creating the earth's vegetation in passing.

At the centre, borne by angels, God is shown wrapped in a swirling mantle, separating the earth from the waters. The foreshortened spiral movement ends in His extended arms stretched over ocean and land. In the corners of this section are four powerful, athletic figures (the so-called Ignudi) who react to the Lord's actions in varying ways.

At the top, in the most famous section, God is enveloped in a shell-like mantle, and, assisted by cherubs, He extends His finger towards Adam. Adam's inert, relaxed body lies in a classic pose, awaiting God's gift of life.

In all three sections, the Almighty is dressed in rosy robes, and other tints are muted. In all of His aspects, God is an explosive force of creative energy and will, amply embodying Michelangelo's powerful conception of spiritual omnipotence.

VII. THE PROPHET ISAIAH; THE ANCESTORS OF CHRIST; THE DELPHIC SIBYL (1508-10)
Fresco.
Vault of the Sistine Chapel

At the left, a meditative Isaiah turns and listens to the cherub whispering in his ear. This figure represents God's voice telling of the coming of the Messiah (Isaiah 7:14). The prophet pauses, gesturing with his left hand. His upper body forms an active counterpoint to his relaxed lower limbs.

In the middle, in one of the eight triangles between the Sibyls and the Prophets, are two of the ancestors of Christ. The man is withdrawn, while the mother protectively shelters her child. Both figures are united in their introspection and solitude.

The Delphic Sibyl is strongly sculptural. Her pose is relaxed, and the drapery is freely treated. She unrolls her scroll with her raised left hand while her right hand rests in her lap. She gazes outward with an intensity tinged with presentiment. Her arms and head are in opposition, a frequent Michelangelesque device. Her vivid red, green and lavender robes are contrasted with Isaiah's green mantle and lilac gown. The white clothing of the figures in the spandrel modulates these stronger colours.

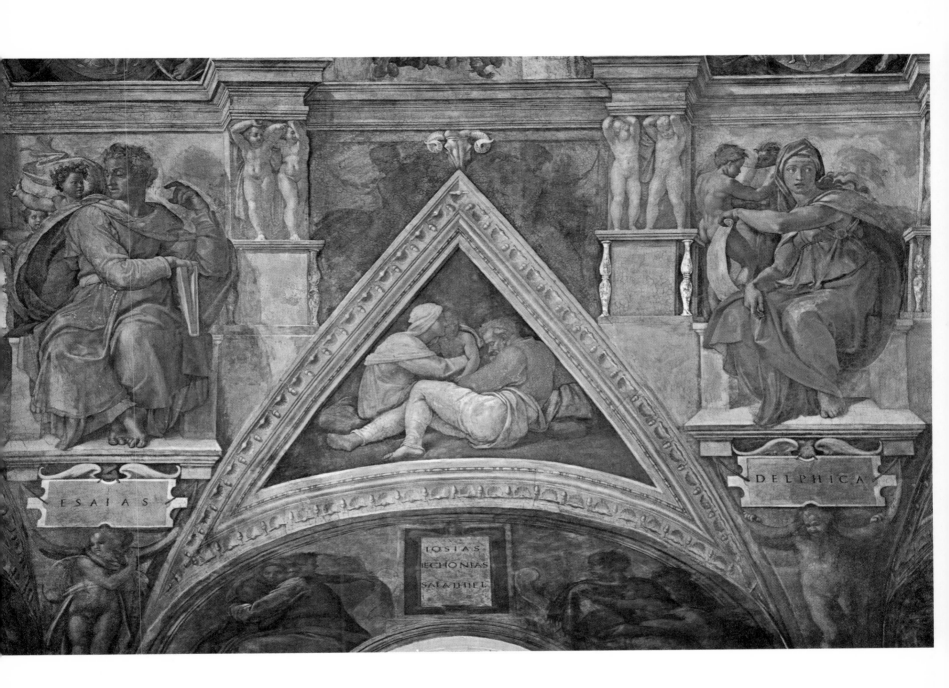

VIII. THE TEMPTATION AND THE EXPULSION
(1509-10)
Fresco.
Vault of the Sistine Chapel

Michelangelo used the tree of knowledge to separate the two dramatic episodes in the Garden of Eden panel. He was the first artist to represent the serpent with a woman's torso. Her long spiralled form is wrapped around the tree, effectively balancing Eve's seductive gesture, reaching upward for the fruit. In Michelangelo's version Adam is as eagerly greedy as Eve, grasping the limb with his left hand while reaching with his right. Seemingly, both are guilty: the man does not have to be coaxed to take the fruit.

In a repeated motif suggesting cause and effect, Adam's extended arm forms one curve when combined with the serpent's reaching gesture. Then, at the right, the thrust of the punishing angel's arm is repeated in Adam's arm reaching back to ward off the judgment.

Michelangelo's concern lies in portraying the dramatic moment, not in creating an idyllic Garden of Eden. The rocky landscape is harsh, and the only sign of vegetation is the leafy limb Adam holds. The palette is neutral. It is significant, however, that the nude bodies are rosier on the left than on the right, where they are tinged with grey to dramatize the fall from grace. The only colourful note is the rose of the angel's robe, which is repeated in the serpent's coils.

IX. THE DELUGE (1508-10)
Fresco
Vault of the Sistine Chapel

Though Genesis suggests a cataclysm, strong seas and heavy rains, Michelangelo depicts mankind's flight from destruction, not the storm itself.

The most crowded episode on the ceiling, this scene is on three different visual planes. The nearest group, on the left, has climbed to the highest point, and these ascending figures are foreshortened. The group on the right rests on a rocky ledge as the waters rise. The background figures in the small, overloaded boat, heading towards the ark, prevent others from climbing aboard. Each group is isolated. The old man carrying his dead son stands separate and poignant.

The figures at the left show the great effort needed to arrive at this temporary refuge. Swirling draperies, which wrap about the figure climbing the tree, are repeated, enclosing mother and child and also the embracing lovers. The angular tent protecting the figures at the right contrasts with the violent activity at the left.

There are isolated touches of vivid colour, but the artist's emphasis is on the contorted sculptural figures. Michelangelo shifts attention from the ark, and the emphasis of Genesis on the survival of Noah, to a sympathetic appraisal of the suffering of those who struggle in vain to escape the deluge.

X. JUDITH AND HOLOPHERNES (1508-10)
Fresco.
Vault of the Sistine Chapel

Michelangelo effectively used the area of this pendentive (triangular piece of vaulting) to tell the story in three distinct segments. The figures of Judith and her maid, in the centre, are executed with clarity of form and colour. Judith looks behind her, and the servant kneels so that Judith may cover the severed head of Holophernes on the tray. At the right, the headless body is still writhing in its death agony. On the left, the guard sleeps, oblivious of the crime.

The poses of the two women are classical, and their garments are sculpturally modelled. The parallel diagonals of their lower bodies are echoed rhythmically by the guard's arms and by the contracting legs of Holophernes. This rhythmic unity, further enhanced by the folds of the drapery at the right, is skillfully underlined by the sharp verticals of the wall against which the women stand.

The red shield of the guard, the maid's golden robe and the rose of the drapery colourfully accent this dramatic scene.

XI-XII. THE LAST JUDGMENT (1536-41)
Fresco.
Altar wall, the Sistine Chapel

Despite Michelangelo's protestation that fresco painting was not old men's work, Pope Paul III insisted the artist undertake the Last Judgment, which took him five years to paint.

This work, covering the entire altar wall, consists of 314 figures in tumultuous motion. All figures, young and old, are athletic nudes. Above, in lunettes on either side, are throngs of angels carrying the instruments of Christ's Passion: on the left, the Cross, and on the right, the pillar where he was scourged.

The middle area represents the kingdom of Heaven. Christ, in a classic pose, raises his right hand in judgment. On His left are the Apostles and on His right, the Patriarchs. Considerable controversy exists, however, as to the individual identities of the various figures.

Angels sound their trumpets while the resurrected bodies at the lower left rise from their graves and ascend towards Heaven. The figures at centre right fall, condemned, to suffer in Hell; some are in the grasp of demons. The spectator's eye is carried from one group to another, in spiral movements from the larger outer circle towards the smaller circle enclosing Christ at the centre.

XIII. DAVID AND GOLIATH (1508-10)
Fresco.
Vault of the Sistine Chapel

There is a striking pictorial unity between these two figures. David raises his sword to sever the giant's head. Goliath twists around to avoid the blow. Both figures are somewhat foreshortened. David's slingshot, with which he has stunned the giant, lies on the ground in front of Goliath.

Michelangelo uses the pendentive form effectively to enclose these figures. Above David, the pink triangle of the tent reverses the architectural form, emphasizing David's upward thrusting arm motion. There is dramatic tension in this gesture, but little anger (I Samuel 17:49).

Goliath wears a moss green cuirass, trimmed with gold, and purple leggings. His white sleeve highlights the arm he uses to raise himself. David's purple sleeve, rose tunic and olive green mantle help tie together background and foreground colours. The two soldiers at the top, right, are incidental to the scene.

David and Goliath were in the part of the Sistine Ceiling Michelangelo painted first, yet even at this early stage the artist succeeded in realizing his dramatic purpose in a rather tight space.

XIV. THE PROPHET JONAH (1511-12)
Fresco.
Vault of the Sistine Chapel

The figure of Jonah, larger than any of the other figures, is situated in a unique position in the chapel—directly below the depiction of God creating light and just above the Last Judgment.

For the artist, Jonah is a dual symbol. Called by God to be a prophet, he first attempted to escape the divine command. Finally, impelled by the implacable will of God, he carried out his mission but remained sullen and rebellious in spirit, complaining bitterly when God's mercy aborted the fulfillment of his prophecy. Michelangelo, himself a revolutionary at heart, was the first painter to portray Jonah's anger. The artist's placement of this symbol of willful disobedience above the main altar of the Sistine Chapel perhaps reflects his own incessant conflict with the Pope during the painting of the ceiling.

Jonah is posed diagonally on his marble seat. His legs are muscular and his chest robust. Rearing backward, he gazes in awe and dismay at the apparition of God above him. The 'great fish', which seems too small to be the one that swallowed him, is placed beside the prophet; behind him is the fig tree.

The remarkable triumph of perspective achieved by Michelangelo in this figure was admiringly described by the early art historian Vasari: 'Who can see without wonder and amazement the tremendous Jonah . . . for the vault, which curves forward, is made by a triumph of art to appear straight through the posture of the figure, which by mastery of drawing, appears to be bending backwards'.

XV. THE PERSIAN SIBYL (1510-12)
Fresco.
Vault of the Sistine Chapel

This aged Sibyl is one of the more poignant figures on the Sistine Ceiling. She is seated at an angle, with her head and shoulders turned away to catch the light as she strains with failing eyesight to read her book of prophecy. Her head is lost in shadow, yet she is clearly very old, with a hump back and gnarled hands. The artist drapes her figure gracefully in fully modelled robes. The deep green of the Sybil's dress becomes a luminous greenish-white in the highlights on the left leg and arm, and this shade is repeated in the turban-like head covering. A lavender mantle falls sculpturally from her shoulder and around her body. The two attending cherubs are almost hidden in shadow.

The Persian Sybil is placed opposite the Prophet Daniel (Cover), and together they flank the Creation (Plate V–VI). The opposition of body and head seen in this pose is a Michelangelesque device used often in his sculptures.

XVI. THE CREATION OF ADAM (1510-11)—*Detail*
Fresco.
Vault of the Sistine Chapel

With these figures of the Lord and Adam, Michelangelo represents the words from Genesis (1:27): 'So God created man in His own image; in the image of God created He him . . .'

The Lord's gesture is superb, as His mighty arm becomes the channel for the life force. Adam's arm, resting passively on his knee, suggests the newness and helplessness of his body before it is infused with life.

Though both the Lord's arm and that of Adam appear similarly muscular and sculpturally painted, Adam's forearm seems soft and flaccid next to the vivid structural strength of the arm and hand of God. Even the colours seem to emphasize this contrast: the tan hue of Adam's flesh seems heavily opaque, while the Creator's arm is rosy and vigourous.

These two figures are the best known of all the Sistine paintings, and justly so, embodying as they have for generations both the majesty and compassion of God in the act of creation.